MEET THE BOLD AND BEAUTIFUL

MAXINE GORDON

ISBN 979-8-9988516-3-6 (Paperback)
ISBN 979-8-9988516-4-3 (eBook)

Author can be contacted via: prophetmax@yahoo.com

Printed in the United States of America

Preface

I was inspired to do a short teaching series on this topic "Meet the Bold and Beautiful"; Then shortly after, I realized that these writings were being developed into a book. As I look around the world today, I've noticed that many persons in this life, have not displayed boldness in its proper form. It may be because of low self-esteem, being an introvert, or something else.

Some folks are very vocal in saying what's on their mind, but when it's time to take action or to execute, very tenuous, weak, and slight feelings manifest. Then there are those who carry out boldness foolishly and unwise. Needless to say, there are many who appear to have a bold front but are weak in some vital areas. I myself realize, that I am not as bold as I thought; There is room for development.

Boldness is having great courage to take on tasks without panicking. Fear is an enemy of boldness. We need more persons who will not shy away from fulfilling their purpose, but those who will see and know that they ought to overcome and win (being bold enough to stand up for what is right and just in society).

I am aware that God made all things beautiful. It was sin that corrupted the human race and caused even the life of man to become ugly and lose its beauty. Because of Christ and His Word, beauty has the capacity to be displayed inside out and restored to us in its natural and spiritual form. Through many encounters, experiences and biblical knowledge, I was able to navigate my way in completing the task (as there were many challenges while writing this book).

Be inspired and encouraged as you maneuver through the journey of the Bold and Beautiful!

Acknowledgments

I dedicate this book to every woman and man who felt crippled in life, drowning by fear, disillusioned, hindered by low self-esteem, and limited because of inadequacy. This book is the rise of your dawning!

My heartfelt appreciation to my family, husband, and children who have helped to highlight the giftings in me. I also acknowledge my colleagues in Ministry, friends, and partners who took time out to intercede and encourage me through the process of writing this book.

However, this could not be possible without my King, Jesus, to whom all Glory belongs.

To my Editor who did an excellent job; Thank you.

Foreword

Life is a journey, filled with expectations and anticipations. What we make of it, is how it treats us. The trajectory God chose for us, it not a misfit or an odd ball. He knows the end from the beginning. Everyone's lives is transparent and visible before His eyes.

While writing this book, I was graced by God with the enablement to use my right hand, albeit I was suffering from a compressed nerve from the neck down to my right arm. But I was reminded that, I can do all things through Christ who strengthens me, and it is by His stripes that I am healed.

Many folks today are not very ardent in fulfilling their dreams, goals and visions, for more than one reason or the other. Some literally have absolutely no desire. This book will attack the fear, doubt, lack of confidence, complacency, sluggard-ness, and low self-esteem. These will no longer be your portion.

Some of you that will be reading this book, have gone through " hell water rise". But it's time to get dressed and stand armed in God's power, arrest Satan and every power from hell, that have been blocking and stopping you. Inside of you is a giant purpose, screaming " let me out"; waiting to manifest.

Just go forth!

Seek God's kingdom and to do His will; living in the standard of His righteousness, standing on repentance ground, and walking blameless. We should be able to glorify God in His made image, because God is the beauty within; Christ in us the hope of Glory.

If we truly cherish Christ, we automatically cherish our body. God made all things beautiful, but sin causes us to see through a different eye. We need to acknowledge entirely, that we were truly created in His pre-possessing, magnificent, drop-dead gorgeous image and beauty, that emanates from those who are truly grateful to be created in God's likeness. Embrace the beauty of Jesus within! Read on!

Table of Contents

Jesus, the Boldest of the Bold

On an unprecedented scale, Jesus went where no man has ever (or could ever have) gone. He went to the Cross to pay that ultimate sacrifice for our sins.

(John 13:1-5) - ***"Now before the feast of the passover, when Jesus knew that his hour was come that he should depart out of this world unto the Father, having loved his own which were in the world, he loved them unto the end. And supper being ended, the devil having now put into the heart of Judas Iscariot, Simon's son, to betray him; Jesus knowing that the Father had given all things into his hands, and that he was come from God, and went to God; He riseth from supper, and laid aside his garments; and took a towel, and girded himself. After that he poureth water into a***

bason, and began to wash the disciples' feet, and to wipe them with the towel wherewith he was girded."

Jesus, being God in the flesh, took a lower position as He chose to wash His Disciples' feet. This happened at a time when most people wore sandals, and their feet would have gotten quite dirty. Persons who would have washed others' feet, would be seen as servants. However, Jesus did this as an example for us to follow. The level of Jesus's humility and love was unrivaled. No wonder Peter told Him that they should be the one washing His feet. **(John 13:6-7 - *"Then cometh he to Simon Peter: and Peter saith unto him, Lord, dost thou wash my feet? Jesus answered and said unto him, What I do thou knowest not now; but thou shalt know hereafter."***

This is the King of kings and Lord of lords (Royalty and Majesty). Just His Posture towards humans would allow Him to transcend beyond borders to show the true nature of His

Father. **(John 5:19) -** ***"Then answered Jesus and said unto them, Verily, verily, I say unto you, The Son can do nothing of himself, but what he seeth the Father do: for what things soever he doeth, these also doeth the Son likewise."*** Truly the Son can do nothing of His own accord, but only what He sees the Father doing. Whatever the Father does, the Son does also.

For Jesus, it certainly was a prerequisite. This showed so much care, love, and empathy. It pictured that they were such a part of Him, in so much, that Peter asked for his hands and head to be washed too. **(John 13:10) -** ***"Jesus saith to him, He that is washed needeth not save to wash his feet, but is clean every whit: and ye are clean, but not all."*** He simply meant those who have received spiritual cleansing. Jesus was referring to Judas' betrayal and Peter's denial. It took great boldness to perceive (for that spur of the moment), that He had to wash the feet of one who would betray Him as well as the other who denied him. Subsequently, their actions would have manifested after this enactment.

Paul said to his followers, 'Follow me as I follow Christ.' (1 Corinthians 11:1). Jesus expects us to even wash our enemies' feet. He wanted us to be bold anyway. I believe that it was also a sign that God would have exalted Him in spite of all of the atrocities. **(Matthew 5:11-12)** – ***"Blessed are ye, when men shall revile you, and persecute you, and shall say all manner of evil against you falsely, for my sake. Rejoice, and be exceeding glad: for great is your reward in heaven: for so persecuted they the prophets which were before you."***

Jesus' Next Level of Boldness

(John 2:15) - ***"And when he had made a scourge of small cords, he drove them all out of the temple, and the sheep, and the oxen; and poured out the changers' money, and overthrew the tables;"*** He cleansed the temple with a whip of chords, overturning tables. A human would have thought that Jesus was malevolent, or evil to perform such an act. He was a Man of Authority and boldness. Instead of assimilating and taking in and understanding the Motive of Jesus' doings (that He is Holy and was manifesting Righteousness to alter the status quo in such a manner), the Pharisees became infuriated. It is in this same breath that we should be bold enough to stand up for what is right.

Jesus was very bold in preaching and teaching the Gospel. He went everywhere with such tenacity, healing the sick, staring at demons in their eyes and casting them out. He spoke intricate things to others. The woman at the well - He had a one-on-one conversation with her, asking questions and answering hers. He was to the point of boldly manifesting the gift of the word of knowledge. Please see 1 Corinthians 12:8 and John 4:5-30.

In Matthew 23:13-39, Jesus boldly dealt with the Pharisees, exercising His authority in such a profound way. ***But woe unto you, scribes and Pharisees, hypocrites! for ye shut up the kingdom of heaven against men: for ye neither go in yourselves, neither suffer ye them that are entering to go in.*** He had no fear speaking the truth in love knowing that His Father was with Him. He knew that the temple would have been destroyed and it would be raised again. He was moving vehemently, spreading the Gospel. Jesus, the Warrior, the Undisputed Champion of Love!

The same commission should be incited in us; stirring up and fanning the flames to witness to the lost and getting them saved (manifesting the character of being bold with wisdom for Jesus).

Personal Anecdote

Growing up was somewhat difficult, because of my tenacious, bold self. This had resulted in me getting more whopping than my siblings. From a tender age I would stand bold enough to back-talk my parents (on occasions) and would stand up for what I believed. It was hard because our parents were not always right, but as a child, your tone should not display the slightest aggression. It always resulted in a good spanking! There were instances where I did not want to have what my siblings had. Maybe I am that type of idiosyncratic person who portrays uniqueness (peculiarity to an extent). '*I am in no way tooting my horn'*.

My boldness continued in my sophomore years in high school, where there were a certain number of cliques present with dominant and manipulative leaders. If you had to join one of those cliques, you would have to go by the books, otherwise you would be dubbed 'an outcast'. As lonely as I thought it would have gotten, I had decided to walk alone. Having a level of boldness in me (that I was not willing to compromise in doing wrong), I rose to the fact that I am a leader and not a follower. This stance that I took resulted in the adopting a tantalizing sort of 'Modus Operandi'. I would then be mocked and teased with such abrasive conduct from the students. It took great boldness to stand up for myself – *'one man against the world'.*

In today's society, so many young people are selling out (compromising); not being able to stand boldly for Jesus (for the truth, the way and life). If you stand for nothing, you fall for everything! **(2 Timothy 1:7)** ***God has not given us a spirit of fear, but of love, power, and a sound mind.*** **(Romans 8:15)** ***"For ye have not received a spirit of bondage again to fear; but ye have received the Spirit of adoption, whereby***

we cry Abba, Father." I never was (and I will never be) perfect, but with having Jesus in my life it is required of me to strive for perfection (maturity and completeness; *James 1:4*). Therefore, I chose not to become a puppet on a string (by God's grace).

There were times in my life when I showed some good amount of boldness. I would speak fluently in small settings but developed wobbled knees in large settings. At the age of 12, I walked boldly with tears streaming down my face to an altar at a crusade, kept by the Blairs (they were known Evangelist at that time). I walked briskly as the salvation call was made, accepted Jesus Christ as my Lord and Savior and felt very excited.

I did not grow up into a Christian home, but used to attend a Methodist Church. That night at the crusade, I saw very small children. Some were weeping and praying in tongues. It was the most beautiful sight I beheld! Immediately, I felt a crave and a strong desire down inside of me, for such an experience. I made that bold step and went home feeling so refreshed and happy to tell my parents the good news. I conveyed to my Mom, what the pastor had told me, that I needed to get be baptized, but she became furious. She told me I was not going to make it! Back then I was angry and felt devasted, because I felt that the strong power of God had moved in my life. I had a true encounter with Christ! For weeks, I vividly remember the impact it had on me. I was broken and felt lonely! I had no one to nurture me, and my mom migrated (shortly after) to the US when I became 14. My neighbor then was very instrumental in encouraging me. God bless her heart - *Ms.Elaine*.

As years passed by, it still lingered in my heart; but finally, my desires were fulfilled as I had recommitted my life to Christ. I realized that my mom then, as intelligent as she was, technically did not understand Spiritual things. Water baptism quickly came into play, along with the baptism of the Holy Spirit. To tell the truth, before water baptism and getting Spirit filled, I struggled intensely after the denial by my parents. But Jesus saves! Being bold for the right reason is glorious!

The definition of boldness is:

1. Show willingness to take risk.

2. Be confident and courageous.

Let's take a journey, in understanding the different characteristics of boldness and how they will impact and enhance our daily walk.

Meet the
Bold and
Beautiful

1

Bold Faith

Now faith is the substance of things hoped for, the evidence of things not seen (*Heb. 11:1*). Faith is believing then seeing! **(Matthew 17:20)** ***"...If ye have faith as a grain of mustard seed, ye shall say unto this mountain, remove hence to yonder place; and it shall be removed."*** Please paint a picture before your eyes. Write the vision **(*Habakkuk 2:2*), (1 Corinthians 16:13) –** ***"Watch ye, stand fast in the faith, quit you like men, be strong."*** Have faith to believe that things will happen.

We have to quit being tenuous (this weak and slight state of being) and take on boldness and tenacity. Even as it relates to our young people, nothing is wrong with saying NO! Say No to illicit sex, drugs, crime, violence, trickery, gangsterism, and the nonsensical patterns of this world. Without faith it is impossible to please God. Faith is now! Young folks, I had to manifest boldness to stop fornicating and doing stuff that was displeasing to my Lord (*Rom 12:1*). God has created my body to offer to him as a sacrifice. My body is God's temple.

If we have the faith to believe (1 *John 5:14*), and this is the confidence we have in him, that if we ask anything according to his will, he hears us. Ask for help! Help! Lord. (*Rom. 4:17*) Call forth the things that are not, as though they were. 'Believe in faith'! I had to start seeing myself being delivered, being freed and blessed by the Almighty God (as I was bound and felt I had curses on my life also). Who the Son sets free, is free indeed!

2

Bold Zeal

Fire to Fulfill

Zeal is passion, fire, appetite, enthusiasm, not logging behind in diligence, fervent in spirit, and serving the LORD (*Rom 12:11*). The Greek word for diligence is spoudazō (making progress, moving ahead). Whether it is your life, business, commitment with God, your family or yourself, we need to carry that fiery zeal to accomplish, fulfill and complete. Cease with the nonchalant behavior (tardy and laid-back posture). Allow a fiery zeal to emanate from your life.

There were certain times when I had become laid-back (in particular, when trials got really heavy). And with this, we tend to shut down or close out. God's word is quick and powerful! Life and Spirit should be lit up with great fervency in our spirits (red hot and on fire!). It burns away complacency and ignites appetites with great exuberance. With expectations, we should burn with bold zeal to accomplish God's work (God's will and purpose for our lives in the Earth).

The Resilient Preacher

The apostle Paul had bold zeal in preaching the mystery of the gospel in chains. He said, I am the called, the chosen in chains, but I will speak boldly the gospel. We have this mandate to preach the gospel in and out of season, 'Rain or Sun'. The Scripture tells us that whatsoever a man's hand findeth to do, do it with all thy might. (*Ecc. 9:10*). The Gospel must be preached to the ends of the Earth.

May God raise up some firebrands who will be soaked in the wisdom and revelation of God's Word with bold zeal and passion, changing and transforming lives. **(Jeremiah 20:9).** ***"Then I said, I will not make mention of him, nor speak any more in his name. But his word was in mine heart as a burning fire shut up in my bones."*** Jeremiah was ablaze to be that mouthpiece for God. May sinners become mesmerized by the fire of God in you, to burn sin out and every carnal weakness.

Please pray this with me - Jesus, if you can use anything, you can use me. Consecrate me to your service for your glory. Amen.

3

Bold Confession

It is a bold admission; owning up (acknowledgement).

(*Matt. 10:32*) Jesus said, if you confess me before men, I will also confess you before my father. Sad to see that many of us put Jesus on a shelf, when sometimes among the unsaved or our peers (even persons of influence and affluent celebrities). Note, Jesus must be the center of our lives! It is him we ought to show off, and not ourselves. He should be on our lips at all times. We should be ready to 'big him up', to exalt, to share him, and be that channel, to decree who he is. Bold confessions of him!

Do it!

(Hebrews 4:16) - "Let us come boldly to the throne of grace, that we may obtain mercy. Greek meaning - obtain, get into, come up with. 'Come, your daddy is waiting'! Come in whatever state you're in. The Greek word for mercy is, Cleo's and it derives from the word olive-oil (widely known for soaking, comfort and healing). God is so compassionate! Just as I am without one plea, his blood gave me the opportunity to gain access. We don't need the devil or anyone's permission. Just note that when you get to God, things change. You will have mighty results!

The Humility Zone

(James 5:16) – *"Confess your faults one to another, … that ye may be healed."* This can be an arduous task as it can be difficult to trust others with our confessions. Albeit it is a requirement by God! Sometimes we appear too high to say I was wrong, or I treated you bad! The Greek meaning for fault is error, mistake, defect, flaw, or blemish. These are what will hinder our prayers from being fervent (Red Hot!). Satan is afraid when we genuinely confess our sins, because when we do so our bodies will be healed (mentally, physically, emotionally, and spiritually); We will even experience financial healing. We will live a very victorious life!

Declare Bold

(*Job 22:28*) We can boldly confess the Word of God over our lives, homes, and family. Whatever we decree, it shall be established. Speak that word! Confess miracles, breakthroughs, open doors, expansion and wellness. Look for establishment, look for growth, and expect it! Believe it! In Jesus name.

Prayer: Dearest Father, closest friend, let the spirit of humility rest upon us. We want to access the great benefits of salvation and be an example in Jesus' name. Amen.

4

Bold Worship

Worship is a lifestyle. **(John 4:23)** – ***"But the hour cometh, and now is, when the true worshippers shall worship the Father in spirit and in truth: for the father seeketh such to worship him."*** Worship is a state of mind, in which we worship with zealousness, creating that atmosphere to worship God every day. That is the intimate communion of incense that flows up to him. The importance of worshipping God is a bold move, reason being that ***"God is a Spirit; and they that worship him must worship him in spirit and truth"*** **(John 4:24)**. The carnal mind has to be subjected, so that the mind of the spirit can touch heaven.

Now more than ever, our worship to God must be genuine; living a double lifestyle is unacceptable! After Jesus ministered to the woman at the well, it was expected of the woman to walk and live a proper lifestyle. This encounter with Jesus, brought her to a place of getting her life and house in order.

Paved Way

Jesus paved the way so that we could live behind the veil. We have received free access through the cross! The absolute legality of entering into his presence is beyond words; 'Free'. Remember in Eze. 28 Satan had all the sounds of heaven in him **(Ezekiel 28:13 – "Thou hast been in Eden the garden of God; every precious stone was thy covering, the sardius, topaz, and the diamond, the beryl, the onyx, and the jasper, the sapphire, the emerald, and the carbuncle, and gold: the workmanship of thy tabrets and of thy pipes**

was prepared in thee in the day that thou wast created.”). He worshiped God in every way and form. The glory of God was all over him. It was his pride that grieved God, he became high minded. God will not share his glory with no man! **(Isaiah 42:8 “I am the LORD: that is my name: and my glory will I not give to another, neither my praise to graven images.”)**. We have to be careful in ensuring to give God all the glory, always. Pride is subtle like a serpent. The more we see ourselves as mere dust and ashes, the more humble we remain. Satan and a third of his angels were kicked out of heaven (and these angels are described as fallen angels, that will try to hinder true worship to God). God is expecting the sweet aroma of worship that will fill his nostrils. The onus is on us to strive to give God our best worship by his Spirit. A right and a contrite heart, God will not despise.

Worship Anyway

Persecution is inevitable, being a true worshipper. Those that desire to live Godly, must suffer persecution. Whatever trials and testing we come up against, must note that your worship is making a difference (creating an atmosphere that will become conducive for miracles and the move of the Spirit). We have to acknowledge him from any vantage point, whether good times or bad times, happy times or sad times. God still expects his honor and reverence. David said, ***"I will bless the Lord at all times: his praise shall continually be in my mouth."*** **(Psalm 34:1)**. May your soul rise and bless the Lord! God will disappoint your disappointers; He will be an adversary to your adversaries and an enemy to your enemies. Worship him in the beauty of holiness. Set the precedence for the next generation and lift up your voice.

Prayer: Precious Jesus we stand to lift and worship your name. You are holy and worthy of our worship. Help us to worship you in Spirit and in truth. We offer our bodies to you, holy and acceptable, which is your reasonable service. May our lives be a worship to you and be filled with you. Amen!

5

Bold in speech (Phil. 1:14)

nd many of the brethren in the Lord, waxing confident by my bonds, are much more bold to speak the word without fear."

Paul's example of imprisonment was a great example of how we are to speak forth the truth in love. Jesus was very bold in speech! It can be quite daunting when you are not allowed to express your opinions, and sometimes there are consequences for being misunderstood. Being bold in speech doesn't mean you are ignorant or disrespectful. Jesus went through it all. Boldness is contagious!

Speak up!

When I was younger, I was told to 'shut up' many times (those experiences diminished my self-esteem). Looking back, I realized that those situations happened because the enemy knew that I would have become a mouthpiece for God. I remember having a spiritual encounter, where I was lying on a bed praying and suddenly, I heard a sound in the Realms of the Spirit and felt a literal force come to my mouth. I felt the impression! If this was physical, my mouth would have been so damaged. I rebuked it in Jesus' name, and it left.

Mouth Catastrophe

On one occasion, Jack and Patsy had an altercation. Jack used to drink quite frequently and would argue a lot [*Note! It is dangerous when men become intoxicated by strong alcohol];* There would always be some sort of uproar. *If you can recall, the old-time enamel jug/pitcher and basin bowl, along with the urinal pan.* Well, in the midst of the uproar, Patsy picked up the jug and flung it at Jack. The sad thing was that I was present at the moment and Jack tried to save himself by picking me up to shield himself. The jug came forcefully at my mouth, blood spewed like water, as two of my teeth fell out. My lips got busted really bad! Folks, the pain was excruciating, and for weeks I wasn't able to eat comfortably, and the rest is history. Looking back, I realize how Satan was after my prophetic calling. He knew that God was going to use my mouth for his Glory. Miraculously my tooth grew back evenly at that age. Glory to God! That was some moment.

Declare with me "MY MOUTH IS A WEAPON AGAINST THE KINGDOM OF DARKNESS, IN JESUS NAME!"

The Power of Evil

Peter and John were imprisoned for preaching the gospel and manifesting the power of God. They were whipped and told to stop preaching. They lifted their hands to God, and uttered, Father behold their threatening's, and grant your servants boldness to speak your word. God, you stretch forth your hands to heal following signs and wonders (*Acts 4:29-30*). Many will be persecuted (not for the enticing speech, but for the revelation and demonstration manifested through the power of the Holy Spirit). Saints "Power and glory will be thy portion".

We must develop that proclivity mindset toward God's end-time strategies while speaking just and bold for Jesus. If you are around someone who is condescending, obnoxious, cynical, and skeptical in their speech, clearly that atmosphere isn't worth it! You don't need them in your circle. Just pray for them! And if we find ourselves with any of these character traits, then deliverance is inevitable. Jezebel falls into this category. Elijah slew her prophets on Mount Carmel, and she was livid (mad); She sent messengers to Elijah to tell him that she was going to kill him. Her words had so many demonic powers that it caused Elijah (a Mighty Man of Valor) to fall into self-pity and loneliness, under a Juniper tree, feeling inferior and unimportant.

Note! Many folks cannot ‘bring forth’ because they are under the spell of Jezebel's threats (this includes Pastors, Leaders, and Church Folk). Now Pastors, you will observe that some people may want to transfer to another church for more reasons than one, or for seemingly no reason at all. Remember! We don't control people's lives. However, the release should be done in decency and in order. If we refuse to give them up and they leave, don't send a sword after them. This is witchcraft along with evil manipulation! We have a slogan in our church. ‘You come, we bless you; You leave, we bless you (if you want the blessing)! If they leave maliciously and out of rebellion, or leave without asking for release, put them in God's Hands and pray for them. ***“For whatsoever a man soweth, that shall he also reap.”*** **(Galatians 6:7)**

There are 7000 that have not yet bowed their heads to Baal! There are so much more fish to scale and fry (metaphorically speaking)!

Jezebel’s plan of demise for Elijah, was overthrown; and in the end it returned on her head. She drank her own blood and ate her own flesh. We have to be careful of the seeds we sow!

Prayer: Jesus, help us to stand up with wisdom and to speak boldly in your name. We cancel every dominant manipulative action or tongue that seek to speak out of biblical terms and context in Jesus’ Name. May wisdom, courage, and strength illuminate our hearts. Amen!

6

Bold Power

Power in the natural sense is the ability to influence or travel with great speed. Also, it is described as a person of great strength (one who expresses bold power in the natural, usually is fearless, tactful, adventurous, and always seems to take on tasks that display impossibility). I remembered when my son Kurtlando was at age seven, he literally went on top of the house (via a ladder), and decided he wanted to jump off to see how powerful he was. My heart felt like it was in my mouth. He actually did it and felt very proud about it too! I was on my way to whop him, but then I realized he had natural abilities and needed proper guidance.

When we think of power (in the natural), we think of electricity, muscles, energy, something explosive and dynamic. All these characteristics of power are somehow positioned in humans and can be executed through various fields. A powerless individual is deemed as being insubstantial, weak, or slight. Accessing 'bold power' begins with the heart and mind. Let's deal with the mind first. A strong mind is better able to process information, make better choices, feel more resilient, and function well in our day-to-day lives. This is also described as a mind that manifests boldness (what you think, the way you think, and what you make of those thoughts in your mind).

Having a bold and powerful heart is more powerful than what the world can throw at you. Boldly facing your giants is more than just you. A heart that is bold with power, expresses courageousness, and can be daring, fearless, not easily panicked, and sticks to the task. We all should exert these different abilities of bold power in a very useful and positive way.

The Negative Side of Power

The occult is the practice of power and knowledge outside of God. For example, witchcraft, divination, necromancy, mediumship, spiritist, parapsychology, telepathy or clairvoyance, observer of times, horoscope, tarot reader, and palm readers. (See *Deut.18:10*) Indulging in the negative side of power, results in your life being cursed, tormented, manipulated by evil deeds, and a big wide-open door to Satan and his demons. We should in no way affiliate ourselves with such. God is light and in him is no darkness. The devil intends to trap the heart, soul, mind, and body of the human. In a great way, God Almighty is pulling humans to light and everlasting life. We therefore have to suit up with the bold Power of God to defeat the evil powers of Satan. The church must carry the power of the Holy Ghost with righteousness and discernment.

Truth be told, some folks had situations where they needed help, went to church and there was no Power of God. Ignorance has led folks to power outside of Christ, because of being desperate for their situation to be better.

If you are reading this book and you're guilty of indulging into any of these practices and you have never repented, get on your knees and ask God's forgiveness. Turn away from such deeds and serve Christ with your whole heart.

Spiritual Power

Jesus said, ***"Ye shall receive power, after that the Holy Ghost is come upon you."*** **(Acts 1:8)**. Power to become.

Accessing bold power, by the Spirit of God, is to witness and to demonstrate the gospel of Jesus Christ. It is power to do the father's will and to do greater works. The Holy Spirit is the Power Source. Jesus went and left the Holy Spirit to equip, transfer and help us to maintain and manifest (through us) God's kingdom here on earth. He is the power that is. Without the Holy Spirit, there is no manifestation of the power of God. We need that spiritual power and working of miracles to cast out devils and to heal the sick and demolish satan's evil schemes.

The Spiritual Power upon God's people cannot be altered or fabricated. The power of God is real and authentic. There is no match (never have and never will be). The devil is afraid of a sold-out (to God) child of God.

Divine Power— 2 Peter 1: 3-4

God in his infinite wisdom would not have left us stranded or in any bemused manner. His bold power enables us to adapt to godly living. There is nothing good about this robe of flesh; The mandate for it, is always to die in God's presence. His power has given us everything we need pertaining to life and godliness. Jesus quoted **(Deuteronomy 30:19)** ***"I have set before you life and death, ...choose life."*** He gave us the most grandiose choice "life" Christ in us is the hope of glory, which also includes, his presence, his power, and his boldness. We will manifest his power in an unmatched way, wherever he would have chosen to use us. High moral standards in our lives, should be the guide to which we exercise Spiritual Power. This power we have to resist to overcome, to stand strong, and to be counted for his glorious return.

Prayer: God you have afforded us natural power abilities and have endowed us with your Spiritual Powers for your work here on earth. Help us to live our daily lives manifesting both for your glory. We resist and cancel every evil power. We shut down, disintegrate and close every door to evil occultism power in Jesus' name. We rebuke it from our bloodlines and speak the blood of Jesus against it. We thank you that whom you have set free is free indeed. Amen.

7

Bold Courage (Gal. 5:1)

***S**tand fast into the liberty to where Christ has set you free. Be no more entangled in the yoke of bondage."*

Stand fast: Firmly remain in position. We are no longer wrapped up in oppressive enslavement. We don't have to go back there! We can develop the bold courage not to dabble anymore. Truth be told, I backslid once, and all hell broke loose. Nothing went well for me. I made it back by God's grace. **(John 10:10) – *"The thief cometh not, but for to steal, and to kill, and to destroy."*** But Jesus comes to give us abundant life. We have God's divine power that gave us everything we need (Please see *2 Pet. 1:3*)

Beat the Odds

I never thought I could truly overcome some hurdles in my life. The word of God became flesh in me (to an extent) and set the precedence for me to believe and accept that God's divine power is in me. Christ in me, the hope of glory (*Col 1:27*) and by God's grace I never looked back. If you have lost your bold courage to keep your integrity, your sanctity and loyalty, 'TAKE IT BACK BY FORCE' in Jesus' name. **(Matthew 11:12) - *"And from the days of John the Baptist until now the kingdom of heaven suffereth violence, [and, men of violence take it back by force]."*** Face up! heads up! I am taking back my bold courage to move forward. Don't go back to that scene - Sleepless nights, that had your pillows wet with tears and extreme discomfort; Humbly reposition and realign.

Your Assignment

Be strong and be of good courage. The Lord goes with thee. You will not fail (*Deut. 31:6*). Your assignment must be executed by bold courage. Queen Esther had an assignment to save her Jewish people. She had to muscle up with extreme doggedness and breach protocols to have the King's Scepter held out to her, to rescue her people from genocide that wicked Haman had plotted against her and her people for their demise. She had no time to become warped in her mind. She had a mission to accomplish, and time was of the essence. I pose a question to you, *"What is that assignment you have that requires bold courage?"* God's promise to you is that you will not fail! Take on that task with great vehemence. Face it! It may seem like a mountain, but in God's eyes it's a plain.

Losing is not an option. The righteous are bold as a lion. Make it! Win! Overcome!

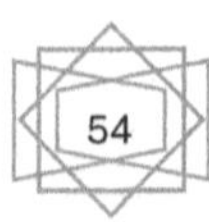

Pass the Past

Joseph was so abused by his brothers but earned the courage to forgive in the end. Sometimes separation is needed for healing and destiny to be fulfilled. He would not have prospered or even be alive around his brothers. God made a way for Joseph's safety. His purpose was too great, and he was the one with the oil of greatness on him. Joseph was surrounded by jealousy which was
considered to be 'as cruel as the grave' and worse than anger; there was also a great manifestation of competition.

The Lonely Walk

Joseph survived all the atrocities he had and was alone in a strange place among strange people.

Sometimes that's how your star will shine. Away from the familiar. Talking about familiarity; You cannot allow your purpose and destiny to be surrounded by people of snake like character (*Not indicating that everyone who is familiar, has a snake like character*). According to Luke 10:19 we should tread upon scorpions and serpents because we have all power over the devil. Those spirits belong under our feet! We wrestle not against flesh and blood, but principalities, rulers of this Dark World (*Eph. 6:12*). Dealing with the demonic spirit in the person or persons, Discernment of the Spirit of God is inevitable. It's wise to know those who are with you and for you. It's also important to possess a positive mindset and stay focused and proactive.

One of my prayers daily is to ask God to keep me from serpent spirits. I remember I used to constantly speak of how I hated snakes. One day God spoke to me clearly, told me that I should not hate what he had created for his pleasure ***(Rev. 4:11*). *'You are worthy or Lord and God to receive glory, honor and power, for you created all things, and for your***

pleasure they were created and exist'. From that day on, I never ever said I hated any creature or animal God has made. However, I truly hate the serpent spirit or demonic spirits that are of the devil. This was a spirit that Joseph's brothers had. Why did such wickedness occur?

They were too familiar with Joseph's prophetic dreams; It definitely breathed contempt (loss of respect). The plan was to shut him down and out so that purpose and destiny dies. Beware! Ensure you are bold and courageous. It was not easy for Joseph to keep the love for his brothers, but he trusted God and was reassured that his destiny was in the hand of God and not his brothers. Different minds, concepts and responses changes things. Sweet! Restoration took place and of course his brothers were sorry for their wickedness to Joseph. If God is for you, then who can be against you! We should treat people with respect. God will exalt them before our faces. Let's live and let others live. For some of us, healing will not come in the same place but will eventually happen. Glory to God on high!

Prayer: Precious Jesus, help us to have the right mindset towards one another. Help us to see them through your eyes - Jesus. Give us the grace to esteem them above ourselves. We trample under feet anything that would seek others demise in Jesus' name. Let the love of Christ shed abroad in our hearts by the Holy Spirit in your precious name.

8

Bold Strength

The Righteous are bold as a lion. It's not easy to stand in the face of danger and still manifest an enormous amount of strength. But it's standing; unwilling to yield and be afraid. (*Isa. 50:7*) Therefore the Lord will help me, I shall not be confounded. I set my face as a Flint (a hard gray rock)! I shall not be ashamed. There were times when God would have set my face hard because of the stand I had to take.

Once, I had gone to the US embassy (located in Jamaica) to apply for a visa. I took my marriage certificate along with other necessary documents. Upon reaching the window where you would have been interviewed, I sweetly said "Good Morning" to the consulate. *You know you definitely would have to tweak that good morning a little*. I handed over my documents and suddenly I saw a change on the consulate's face. I became curious because her smile went, and I was now looking at her peeved facial expression, annoyed and seemingly disgruntled. I kindly asked her "Ma'am is everything OK?" Suddenly she shoved my documents to me, looked into my face and let me know that I will not be able to travel to the United States, ever. She didn't give me a chance to say anything. She had only stamped my book, DENIED! And 'the cheek of it' (an English term), she had used a red ink pen to further the damage. She told me my marriage certificate was fraudulent. I stood there (being appalled) and I panicked a bit, as she was quite daunting, repulsive and rude. I gently collected my documents, told her thanks and left the building. Truth be told, I felt like God was somewhere in this, because my document was quite legit. The process would have been to have the documents verified in two weeks and transported by two members of the Jamaica Defense Force. I eventually got in touch with the head of the US Embassy department, a gentleman who was so gracious and willing to hear my story. The end of the two weeks appeared, and I told him that my certificate was authentic. Then I was summoned back to the embassy to collect my visa. *'Tell me who was at the window?'* The same consulate who thought my destiny was in her hand. She broke out into a very wide smile as she hurriedly handed me my 10-year visa and apologized. I took it gracefully, said thank you and gave a faked smile. I wasn't angry, but it wasn't an easy pill to swallow. It is so ironic that people can declare boldly what will happen to your future, as if it's in their hands. I had felt strength through the denial. I was cognizant of the fact that God would have fought this for me. Well, he surely did! Note! What is yours, is yours! The gates of hell shall not prevail. Don't let anyone talk you out of your bright future. (*Jer. 29:11*) The plans I have is to prosper you and not to harm you. Look out for God's glorious opportunities for your life!

There were a few moments during the process I felt a bit Melancholy, reason be, I was just pulled out of a bank job for full time ministry. How cool was that? *Intimidation can break your strength and lower your self-esteem, but being with God in challenging times greatly encourages us.* We are to become strong in the Lord and in the power of His might (*Eph. 6:10*), embracing God's empowerment and relying on God's presence in everything we do; that He may grant us according to the riches of His glory (God's riches of goodness), to be strengthened with might by His Spirit. *'Let the weak say I am strong'*. We need bold strength to rise, to run this race with patience, to eat right, exercise and nourish that golden body of ours. Get rest, good sleep and keep a good spirit.

Prayer: Lord, I receive strength to run through a troop and leap over walls and hurdles that would face me. I manifest bold strength to fulfill my call in Jesus' name.

9

Bold Prayers

Let us come boldly to the throne of grace that we may obtain, acquire, gain, and lay hold of mercy (*Heb. 4:16*). Mercy cannot be issued inside of a bad heart. Come boldly in prayer at all times. God doesn't require us to be afraid, but rather to fear Him! There were times in my walk with God that I was afraid to face him because of sins, not realizing how great his mercy was to me.

Avoid Prayer Frights

We were all called to pray. The way to advance in your prayer life and receive boldness is to:

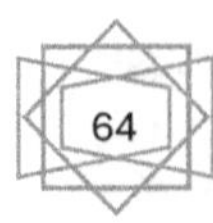

1. Spend time in God's presence
2. Study scriptures
3. Allow the Holy Spirit to have his way in your prayer time and pray sessions

In other words, pray Spirit-led prayers. (*Jam. 5:16*) The effectual fervent (hot!) prayers of a righteous man availeth much.

It is very sad when you call on an individual to pray and there is no power, no fire in their prayers, along with no intelligence/knowledge. Frights come in when we don't soak in his presence. The most powerful prayer you can pray, is praying back God's Word to Him.

Prayer and Victory Process

(Revelation 8:3-5) – ***"And another Angel came and stood at the altar, having a golden censer; and there was given***

unto him much incense, that he should offer it with the prayers of all saints upon the golden altar which was before the throne." **(Vs 4) -** ***"And the smoke of the incense, which came with the prayers of the saints, ascended up before God out of the angel's hand."*** **(Vs 5) -** ***"And the Angel took the censer, and filled it with fire of the altar, and cast it into the earth: and there were voices, and thunderings, and lightnings, and an earthquake."***

The golden censer was to penetrate God's presence with incense. The incense is the precious pleasant prayers up to heaven. The golden altar is Christ's ongoing intercessory work of prayer. These prayers that were thus accepted in heaven, produce great changes in the earth. The same Angel that placed the prayers of the Saints into the censer, took the fire from the censer and released it into the earth. There were strange noises, thunder, lightning and earthquakes. These were the answers, God gave from the prayers of the Saints. It was a symbol of his anger against the world - that he would do great things to avenge Himself and his people from their enemies.

Prayer Bolts

Men and women in the Bible prayed bold prayers. Joshua prayed that the sun would stand still. Elijah prayed that it would not rain in the earth for 6 months and 3 years. Daniel, David, and Esther, when certain occasions arose, they knew it was time for bold prayers. The Scripture declares that when the enemy comes upon you like a flood, the Spirit of the Lord raises up a standard against him (Isa 59:19). The Holy Spirit raises up a standard by providing spiritual protection, when we work in harmony with God and by empowering believers to stand against spiritual attacks. It's God's revelation to us about the enemy.

Folks, you just can't sit by and allow the enemy to win. He is already a loser, and he wants to take you out! He is after our families, friends, the ministry, your money, and your anointing. Be a step ahead through bold and anointed prayers. Manifest your God-given rights and authority. Always strike the iron while it is hot. Pray bold prayers over your dreams and visions. The devil's trying to hinder you, to deny you and your family. Release bold prayers. Turn on the heat!

Prayer: Heavenly Father, I thank you for the process to which you present our prayers in heaven, Lord, cause our prayers to continue to be an incense unto you that will result with great victories.

10

Bold Warnings

But truly I am filled of power by the Spirit of the Lord, and of might to warn and to declare to Jacob his transgression and to Israel their sins **(*Isa. 58:1*). (Ezekiel 33:6) - *"But if the watchman sees the sword come, and blow not the trumpet, and the people be not warned; if the sword come, and take any person from among them, he is taken away in his iniquity; but his blood will I require at the watchman's hand."***

If we indeed fail to warn folks about evil deeds and unholy lifestyle that will destroy their lives; If we fail to warn them about the consequences of not accepting Jesus Christ as their personal Lord and Savior (telling them about the impending judgment, heaven and hell, life after death); If we stand back and be silent; Their blood will be on our shoulders.

In society today, so much corruption is in the air (in our country and countries around the world). Heads of Government are involved in nepotism, moral decline, muzzling, and the list goes on. Anything goes! It's about selfish gains and ambition (even if someone's head has to be walked on); Whatever the means and through whatever mediums. Evil portals are opened by cults and the occult. These kinds of patterns and practices are even capturing the minds of the young, and will invoke God's punishment and judgment. We have to constantly blow the prayer trumpet strategically!

The Church has the answer!

We should by no means bow or succumb to these wrongheaded contrary leadership patterns. The Lord has taught us to esteem highly those who have the rule over us but not to compromise with corruption. As a church, we stand cowardly not being able to 'call a spade a spade' anymore. Many have been bribed and threatened! Others have lost the willpower to stand for or stand against. We have the keys to the Kingdom. Our voice as the church must be heard and must be used as a channel to funnel the gospel of Jesus Christ (through the justice system), and to stand up for what is known to be right in the sight of God. God is merciful, compassionate, slow to anger, and plenteous in mercy, but He is also a man of war and a consuming fire.

I remember then, and sometimes even now, when I felt like Micah in the Spirit (The Spirit of truth, might and Judgment would come upon me). This kind of grace attracts enemies and is sometimes a lonely walk. I rested upon this scripture (*Col. 3:3*) that my life is hid in Christ. The Lord wants us to be sober (sensible and vigilant), for the enemy is like a roaring lion seeking who he may devour. May we never compromise, not even with our own self. May that cry come up within us (for righteousness) that will exalt a nation; For sin is a reproach.

Prayer: I pray that the Spirit of Micah be released in your life, to bring godly order in your houses, your church, and in the nations of the earth. Let the Spirit of bold warning manifest powerfully with love and wisdom, in this end time in Jesus's name. Amen.

11

Bold to Succeed

The Israelites went to spy out the land. They were twelve (in number), and ten came back with an odious report. But Joshua (the son of Nun) and Caleb (the son of Jephuneh) came back with a preeminent report, stating that the land that God has given to them was exceedingly good. This was a sure promise to them, a land flowing with milk and honey. The Hebrew meaning for Joshua is 'God of salvation' and 'God is deliverance'. Joshua's life was destined to succeed. The name Caleb in Hebrew means 'bold', 'brave', and 'wholehearted'. It tells me that they were willing to take it by force; that these men were of a different kind.

These two men stood ardent and firm towards the fulfillment of prophecy. They could have believed a lie or doubt God. But the prophecy was given for them to possess the land no matter what. They had displayed boldness to succeed. The other spies saw themselves as mere grasshoppers, insignificant and unimportant. The giants in the land brought them to a state of being petrified. The display of their mundane character was solely because of their mentality (this was clearly blocking their blessings). Note! We have to believe God's word over our sight. Joshua and Caleb were immovable and unshakable in their thinking.

How powerful and tenacious are you in your thought patterns? How bad do you want to captivate the fulfillment of your prophecy? How fervid are you willing to become to accomplish bold success? God is not slack concerning His promises. The weapons will form but will not prosper. Storms will come, but you can ride over them. Mountains will become plains, and valleys will be exalted. Goliaths and Jericho walls will fall. Hallelujah!

Being in limbo and doubt should not be your portion. It's time to pivot, adapt and adjust. Create fundamental change in your life and head to your Promised Land. All God's promises are yes and Amen! His Word has gone forth over your life. Develop a 'win' mindset. Create the atmosphere of being bold to succeed.

Wealth Journey

The greatest of success is to fulfill your God-given assignment and purpose here on Earth. Perseverance, positioning, and aligning oneself is inevitable. One of our own Jamaican born billionaire, Mr. Lee-chin, tells how he lived a risked-filled life to create generational wealth. His upbringing was humble (being an adopted child). He disclosed that he was a starving student, which led him to reach out to the Jamaican government who offered him stewardship, and he received five thousand per year. He continued to share the difficulty he had securing a job suited for his qualification. His persistence allowed him to send out 100 resumes for an Engineering job, and in return he received 100 rejections. These rejections instilled a drive and a boldness to succeed from deep within. He had started to wonder how he could make people's lives wealthy (who had helped him along his life's journey). Now he is Michael Lee-Chin, OJ, OOnt a Jamaican billionaire businessman, philanthropist, holding INC, and the list goes on. He simply saw how he could make others' lives better, including his and his family. He took the trajectory; took it all with great vehemence.

Let's look at another one of Jamaica's legends. The Hon. Usain Bolt. He started with nothing. From a humble childhood in Jamaica, he pushed his way to victory through great courage, hard work and determination. I can imagine he had some setbacks and challenges, but he was determined to beat all odds (including others on the field). One of his mottos is "focus on what you need, pay the price, it will be worth it all". He made all Jamaicans proud, including the rest of the world. He wasn't born long legged for nothing - as he was destined to be a champion (to lift his life and family from a humble start to a multi-millionaire status). Usain left an indelible mark on most, if not all of us. He lifted the hopes and dreams for every aspiring athlete. He was 'dubbed' the greatest runner of all times.

Brain Cells Acceleration

You can be who you were destined to be:

1. Believe in yourself
2. You can do those projects

3. Manifest those dreams and goals (Focus)
4. Be that Coach- that Entrepreneur
5. Produce that next song
6. Enter that new career
7. Write that next book
8. Beat the Odds
9. Change the Status quo
10. Write that positive affirmation about yourself

Today many have taken a page out of Mr. Lee-Chin and Usain's book. Subsequently they would have followed suit, adopting that same drive, passion and purpose to win, fulfill and complete.

Having said all of this, there are many bible characters who went from rags to riches (Father Abraham, Esther, Joseph and Moses). If our wealth and gifting is not impacting others' lives, particularly our family, then I believe we are not wealthy yet! Abraham carried generational wealth. What are you carrying? How are you handling your gifts, talents and purpose that you were created to manifest and fulfill. The process is quite tedious and sometimes strenuous, but the outcome is glorious. Live and let others live! Think big, think large, think mighty, think consciously, think wisdom, think honestly, and think powerfully.

Prayer

Blessed Jesus, we have not received the spirit of bondage to fear, but we have received the Spirit of adoption, whereby we cry Abba Father. Help us to take on the boldness to succeed in every area of our lives. You are a God of divine strategies and a man of your Word. Make us tolerant in this end time so there may be torrential flow (to change and impact this generation in a great way) in your name, Amen.

12

Bold Love

G***reater love hath no man than this, that a man lay down his life for his friends."*** **(John 15:13)**

It's like dying to self so others may live (Sacrifice). The Agape is the highest form of love (charity) and the love of God for a human being, and of a human being for God. ***"God so loved the world, that He gave his only begotten Son [*****'offered him up' and 'abandoned self'*****], that whosoever believeth in Him should not perish, but have everlasting life"*** **(John 3:16).**

I reminisce on the songwriter's words, "The love of God is so rich and pure oh measureless and strong".

The first commandment is to love the Lord with all thine heart, and with all thy soul, and with all thy mind. This is the first and greatest commandment, Agape! And the second is to love thy neighbour as thyself (Greek: “Philia” - love others; “Philautia”- love self).

We are living in a world where selfishness breeds so much hate and evil. The love of many have waxed cold. Lives doesn't matter anymore; Human beings (now more than ever) have become baits for heinous crimes and violence. It’s palpably clear that Jesus, the one who so love us, will be returning soon. Paul in (*2 Cor. 7:3-4*) said, you are in our hearts to die and to live with you. “Philia” was the measure of love he had for them, even though he had to rebuke in love at times (nowadays when you give a simple rebuke, you are seen as unlovable). Please read in Scripture how many times out of Jesus's love he had to rebuke, reproof, correct, and let alone encourage.

There is no one under the sun that loves as He does. Jesus taught us to love our neighbors as ourselves. Our neighbors are anyone around us, regardless of their ethnicity, religion or social economic status. A lot of times we say we love, but love demands action - not just mere words. It also requires attention. If you are married and all the man and the woman needs is only to satisfy each other's sexual needs, that's not love in completion. So much more is required! This is one of the reasons God told the man to 'love your wife as Christ loved the church, and gave himself for it'. Love her according to knowledge. What is knowledge? Knowledge are truths that God commands, wants us to know, believe and heed. **(1 Peter 3:7) "Likewise, ye husbands, dwell with them according to knowledge, giving honour unto the wife, as unto the weaker vessel [in strength], and as being heirs together of the grace of life; that your prayers be not hindered."** Your prayers will not be answered! I Ask this question - *Which human being on the face of this earth, is not eager to have* *their prayers answered by God?* Men are to love their wives by the soul help of the Holy Spirit. It is different if you have decided to part ways, and that intimate-love side of you has dissipated. However, love is still inevitable (even as friends).

Wives ought to love and submit to their husbands as doing it unto the Lord (*Eph. 5:22*). That word submission means 'to bend' to authority. It's to deploy oneself in service. Iron sharpens Iron! By no means, I am trying to justify anything - but I believe this saying, 'Happy wife, happy life!' The truth is, a wife has to value herself even through hard times in the marriage. Both are responsible to make each other feel special and appreciated. A man wants respect, a woman needs love, honor and attention. These are seals that foundationally help to hold the marriage together along with intimacy. If these seals are broken, and not repaired then the marriage will have a precarious fall.

Win Love

It is impossible to love without Christ. Christ is love, and in him is no hate (only for sin!). We can do all things through Christ, who strengthens us. We can love from our hearts. Christ, he is within us, the hope of glory (*Col. 1:27*). Above all, love each other deeply, because love covers a multitude of sins (*1 Pet. 4:8*). Peter was reminding us of how we are all forgiven; Christ's death atones! Not one of us would stand in God's presence without condemnation, if it wasn't for the blood. Love! love! love, with Christ!

Prayer: Heavenly Father, help us truly to love from the heart. Your sacrifice was an atonement for hate. You made the greatest exchange ever. May our love increase for you more and more and for others in Jesus' name, Amen.

13

Jesus Most Beautiful

He is the radiance of the glory of God, the exact imprint of his nature, and he upholds the universe by the word of his power. After making purification for sins, he sat down at the right hand of the Majesty on High (that beautiful splendor emitted from a luminous body). When I think of His Majesty, such impressive beauty, our King, our Master and Lord; His magnificence and his gorgeousness - No wonder the scripture says he made all things beautiful (because it's only beauty that lies in him). A glimpse of heaven and the beauty of the earth is enough to tell of his éclat.

(Psalm 50:2) – ***"Out of Zion, the perfection of beauty, God hath shined."*** The beauty that is stunning and strikes our hearts with delight. The songwriter says, "Let the beauty of Jesus be seen in me". Lord help me to carry your beauty in the earth, in every aspect of my life.

Let the beauty of God be upon us and establish our hands (*PSM 90:17*). Oh, we need beautiful hands to do His work for His glory! The beauty of God is truly about His excellence. **(Psalm 27:4) – *"One thing have I desired of the Lord, that will I seek after; that I may dwell in the House of the Lord all the days of my life, to behold the beauty of the Lord, and to enquire [meditate] in his temple."*** It is distinct, that the beauty of God is arrayed in his temple! God can take what the devil has marred (a situation that has been disfigured) and make something beautiful out of it.

In that day, the Lord of Hosts will become a beautiful crown and a Golden Diadem, a Badge of Royalty, a bind rounded to the Remnant of his people. MOST BEAUTIFUL SAVIOR! Your eyes will see the King in his beauty; they will behold distant land (*Isa. 33:17*). His beauty will dispel power to keep us safe, and our faith in the beauty of His power will keep us long.

Beautiful is defined as attractive, pretty, handsome, drop dead gorgeous, pulchritudinous, or Heavenly.

Jesus made all things beautiful. Truly it's because of the sin of Adam and Eve, why things or people are seen as being ugly. Albeit what one man finds beautiful, the other may not, as the perception of beauty is subjective and depend on individual taste. The sin caused us to look through the eyes of the flesh. The Word of Jehovah (God) stands!

I used to sing this hymn at school – "All things bright and beautiful, all creatures great and small. All things wise and wonderful, the Lord God made them all." Beauty is in the eyes of the beholder!

Sin entered the world through one man. This allows us to work out our own salvation with fear and trembling (working on the inner man through the Resurrection Power of Jesus Christ). (*Prov. 18:14*) The spirit of a man sustains him, but a wounded spirit who can bear?

Let's begin with the inner beauty

14

Beautiful in Spirit

1 Peter 3:3-4

The challenge - Your beauty should not come from the outward adornment (braided hair, gold jewelry, or fine clothes). This is expensive! It should be one of the inner self, the inner man (that unfading beauty that is not liable to be forgotten or dismissed, but rather unforgettable, gentle, and a quiet spirit which is of great work in God's sight). The scripture is basically saying that it is not how we are adorned on the outer that makes us beautiful, but it's what lies in the inner core of our being. It's possessing a meek, quiet and cool spirit (which is of understanding), and a calming force in different situations.

For example, it's never easy when a loud voice is on top of yours (whether it's a male or a female), but it's no longer 'an eye for an eye' or 'a tooth for a tooth' that justifies how people should be punished, but moreso according to the way in which they offend. Self-control is in inescapable. (*1 Sam. 16:7*) But the Lord said to Samuel, do not look at his appearing height or his stature because I have rejected him. For God sees not as how men see. Man looks at the outer, but God looks at the heart. Clearly Saul was a tall handsome – good looking man, but his spirit was not beautiful. He went after David with such hate. He abhorred David to the core because of the doors of disobedience that Saul himself opened. He had a strong spirit of jealousy, competition and strife mixed with pride.

Saul was always making excuses for his actions; So it is with us when we do wrong. Instead of humbling ourselves, we justify our actions and tend to hate others. Saul had serious past issues that caused him to send a javelin at David. Sometimes when people want to get rid of you, they do bad things to you. He didn't have the guts to tell David to his face how he despised him, so he acted out his disrelish. There were times in my life when I felt hate because of the many injustices that were done to me, but I had to find ways (in God) to heal my spirit. It took me to a place of hot pursuit, relentlessly seeking the help of the precious Holy Spirit to feed my thoughts and mind with good, so that my spirit would soar. The Word of God made even greater sense in my situation. (*2 Cor. 4:16*) Thou the outer man perishes while the inner man is renewed day by day. The Word of God stands forever! **(Matthew 5:8) – *"Blessed are the pure in heart: for they shall see God."***

Godly Posture

David had a responsibility to not allow Saul's viciousness to attack or affect him anymore. He had times when he could have retaliated, but God!

(Proverbs 20:22) – *"Say not thou, I will recompense evil; but wait on the Lord, and he shall save thee."*

The spirit of a man is the lamp of the Lord. Searching all the innermost parts of the being, a person's spirit illuminates who and what they really are. God will lead you by His Spirit. When you hear and see people's actions day to day, you can tell what is in their spirits (whether it's bad or good, wicked or evil). The devil wants to trap your spirit, so it won't display beauty. A beautiful spirit is beauty to the body and is respectable and decent to God.

Prayer: Jesus, thank you for the work of the Cross. Thank You for helping us to create beauty in our spirits. We yield to You, withholding nothing. We give You glory, in Jesus' name, Amen.

15

Beautiful Conversation

Let your conversation be always full of grace, seasoned with salt, so that you may know how to answer everyone (*Col. 4:6*). It's speaking with kindness, patience, and reflecting God's love, speech that is wise, tasteful, edifying and preserve good relationship. Our words should be of great taste and delight to people who hear them. Develop an utterance to speak as we ought to speak. It really has to do with prudent and decent conduct. **(1 Corinthians 15:33)** – ***"Evil communications corrupt good manners."*** (*Eph. 4:29*) Let no unwholesome, noxious, poison or unpleasant word proceed out of your mouth, but only for edification and building according to the need of the moment. Malicious gossip, defamatory talk, calumny throw words and smeared words (that would attack persons character) should not be our options.

Eat Sweet

If we are going to allow our conversations to make a difference in society, then we have to carry the aroma of sweet words in our mouth. **(Proverbs 16:24) –** ***"Pleasant words are as an honeycomb, sweet to the soul, and health to the bones."*** One of the reasons why bones are unhealthy are because some of the unpleasant words that comes out of the mouth are formed in the heart. (Luke *6:45*) Out of the abundance of the heart, the mouth speaks. This also gives arthritis (bone disease). Some persons swear a lot (it is their daily bread). It's like bitter poison that spreads and affects our health. The proverbs tell us about the wonderful values and benefits of speaking pleasant words. God blesses the souls and the bones of the body (Prov. *16:24*). With long life I will satisfy you and show you my sweet salvation (*PSM 91:16*)

We have to repent (turn from and change our pattern of speaking by the help of the precious Holy Spirit). Have you ever heard this term, "Sweet Spirited"? It's definitely because someone got their conversation right! Our conversation can either be for a blessing or a curse. Choose to bless!

Restrain It

(*Prov. 17:27*) He who restrains/holds back his words have, knowledge. Knowledge is power; it's intelligence. Both the intellectual and the not so intellectual can end up speaking too much (too talkative). Sometimes persons like these cannot be trusted. Speaking hastily will fall short!

(*Prov. 25:11*) Like golden apples set in silver is a word spoken at the right time (this is like persons who just know what to say at the right time). Imagine a golden apple in silver, how beautiful would that sight have been. So would be your vision, your secret, or your story, spoken to the right person at the right time. You will put your opponent to shame when you are sound in speech. It is beyond reproach (*Titus 2:8*). It's the place to be! Beautiful conversations.

Prayer: Heavenly Father, help us to develop sweet conversations in our mouths, as it is for blessing and not for cursing. Cause our words to be preserved by salt so lives will be changed, and our enemies be put to shame in Jesus' Name. Give us wisdom of who to share our visions, dreams, and secrets to (as a means of acquiring genuine and godly support). These mercies we ask in Jesus' Name, Amen.

16

Beautiful Soul

Psalm 50:2

So very often you would come across these words "beautiful soul". It's having a life of spiritual fullness, not just material possession or worldly success. Making sure the soul is saved for Christ return. It is a flame that throws light on people who would have engaged you. The Hebrew word for soul is "Nephet" and it means to break! Out of Zion, the perfection of beauty has come. The perfection of beauty is when God shines in radiance when the soul begins to glow. Note, the soul is breakable! (*Gen. 2:7*) God breathed into man and he became a living soul. You see, man is merely a lump of dirt. God breathe into that lump of dirt, transforming it into a living soul.

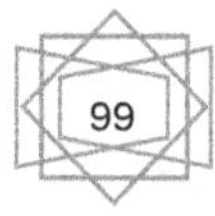

The soul is made up of man's will, intellect, and emotions. The spirit is the part to which men communicate with the spirit realm. The body communicates with the physical realm, and the soul is between these two. **Note,** Satan is interested in taking the soul that had received the Breath of God! If the Breath of God is removed from our body (the lump of dirt), we will die. **(John 10:10) –** ***"The thief cometh not, but for to steal, and to kill, and to destroy: I am come that they might have life, and that they might have it more abundantly."***

Help the Soul!

(Psalm 19:7) – ***"The law of the Lord is perfect, converting the soul: the testimony of the Lord is sure, making wise the simple."*** The law has its authority and all its excellency from the Law Maker. The Law of the Lord is perfect. It is perfectly free from all corruption. It is perfectly fitted for that which it is designed, which makes the Man of God perfect (nothing to be added or subtracted). It converts the soul and brings us back to ourselves, to God, to our duty. The law shows us our sinfulness and misery (our departure from God and the indispensable necessity to return to Him). The soul of man has to be healthy and protected to function accordingly. **(Psalms 116:7) –** ***"Return unto thy rest, O my soul; for the Lord hath dealt bountifully with thee."*** Be healed, be delivered, be set free!

Soul Praise

(Psalm 103:1) - "*Bless the Lord, O my soul: and all that is within me, bless his holy name.*"

The soul cannot bless the Lord when weights are on it. David said, (*Psm.84:2*) 'My soul longed and even yearned for the courts of the Lord. My heart and my flesh sings for joy.' The soul must constantly yearn for God and His Presence to keep it longing for more and free from bondage and sin. We have a voice and God has ears. Cry out like David, **(Psalm 138:3)** – ***"In the day when I cried thou answeredst me, and strengthenedst me with strength in my soul."*** On the day I called, You answered me; You made me bold in strength in my soul (the constant keeping of a Beautiful Soul)! I heard this saying once, that 'the eye of a man can tell what's in his soul'. I believe somehow, it is true. On occasions looking in the eyes of persons, I could tell (by discernment) things that trapped in their soul (lust, lies, deceit, evil, jealousy, and much more). Whether it be Christian or none-Christian. It's highly important to have a serious prayer- life in God! Many times I've seen these played out. Guard the soul!

Prayer: Precious Holy Spirit, help us to pray more for the souls of men. Lord Jesus, teach us how to develop healthy and beautiful souls, and to guard from the evil one who comes to steal, kill, and destroy and from the corruptions of this world. Help us to feed it with love for You and Your Presence. Cause our souls to be actively worshipping You and panting after You daily, in Jesus' Name, Amen.

Cleanse Me – Emotions

The emotion is a strong feeling. It derives from moods and situations. It's also intuitive, sensational, and reactional. Out of the emotion derives pain, bitterness, wrath, malice, strife, and the list continues. Can you remember that old song - 'it's just emotion that's taking me over, tied up in sorrows, lost in my soul'? The emotions can be tied up by dangerous ill feelings. You can actually be at a place where you feel like you cannot control the emotions. (*Ecc. 11:10*) So remove grief and anger from your heart and put away pain from your body. This shows us that we have work to do! To bring our emotions under control, the sooner we acknowledge that our emotions are in turmoil, we can repent and seek God's help!

(*Mal. 4:2*) For the Sun of righteousness shall arise with healing in his wings/beams, and ye shall grow up as calves of the stalls. The "Sun" is referring to Jesus, who will arise and heal you with His Healing Light; Then you will begin to mature in your emotions. Praise Jesus! Hallelujah! I remember when my emotions were out of control. But God! Even now and forever I will have to guard it well and bring it under subjection. Guard it well!

Free the Mind!

The intellect is a part of the soul "Neron" which means reasoning, mental power, a thinker, or a clever person. When this area of our lives is developed and subjected to the Holy Spirit, godly

wisdom flows instead of man's wisdom (which is foolishness in God's Sight). **(1 Corinthians 3:19) –** ***"For the wisdom of this world is foolishness with God. For it is written, He***

taketh the wise in their own craftiness." Outside of this, it's easy for anyone to be seen and act as an intellectual fool, know-it-all, prideful, or narcissistic person. Paul says in **(1 Corinthians 2:4-6) -** ***"And my speech and my preaching was not with enticing words of man's wisdom, but in demonstration of the Spirit and of power: That your faith should not stand in the wisdom of men, but in the power of God. Howbeit we speak wisdom among them that are perfect: yet not the wisdom of this world, nor of the princes of this world, that come to nought:"***

Total dependence on God is Beautifully Intellectual!

17

Beautiful through Trials

The three Hebrew boys, Shadrach, Meshach and Abednego faced many afflictions by king Nebuchadnezzar. They had refused to bow down to their god or allow the

manipulations of the king to deter them from reverencing the true and living God. The three Hebrew boys had a relationship with God. Daniel, in particular, had a committed prayer life. Therefore, they remained poised, prayerful and purposeful. It's as a result of their posture and how God fought for them that the king came to the understanding that these guys God is real and should be reverenced (even though he persecuted them time and time again). When your enemies come face to face with God, their knees will bow, and their tongue will confess. God will show himself strong and mighty on your behalf.

How about you? Do you leave the throne room while you are being persecuted? Or it is that you offer up more incense to God in prayers and worship, and trust God to take you through? **(2 Corinthians 4:8-10)** – ***"We are troubled on every side, yet not distressed; we are perplexed, but not in despair; Persecuted, but not forsaken; cast down, but not destroyed; Always bearing about in the body the dying of the Lord Jesus, that the life also of Jesus might be made manifest in our body."*** It's the assurance we have in Christ and his word; the spectrum light that brings out the beauty in us like a rainbow (The colors of God's "Agape" love for us, colors of our trust in him, colors of hope, colors of strength and endurance, and colors of peace and settlement". He is that light within us, through our roughest and darkest hour.

There were moments in my walk with God, even being married to a Pastor, I faced unbearable trials and persecutions, that drove me close to suicide. The affliction that men sometimes put on you can be so malevolent, demonic and wicked (driven by the flesh and the works of darkness). There were times when I had to pretend (for the sake of my family and members). It was that light spectrum that radiated from the love of Jesus, allowing that light to penetrate spirit, soul, mind, and heart. Being a worshipper and a song writer, I had to remember that God is first (in front of every trial) and knows the end from the beginning. My worship evoked the Resurrection Power of Jesus Christ, and it came with such power that the suicidal thoughts were annihilated and put to flight (Glory to Jesus). He is the light, and in him there is no darkness. Having said all of that, healing took time to complete.

Don't allow anyone to manipulate your healing process. Some healings are gradual (even after forgiveness). When Christ appears on a scene, he exposes darkness. He appears with a dragnet to trap the enemy on your behalf, while Christ gently leads you out in a timely manner.

18

Beautiful Tongues

Greatness cost! On several occasions through trials, the model of my prayers was praying in tongues. My strength was not mustered for English. My prayer language was inevitable (Jude 1:20) Stir up the gift in you in the most Holy Faith, by praying in the Holy Ghost. The out of belly experience causes you to communicate with God without Satan's knowledge. Praying in the Spirit kept me in constant connection with God (whenever my spirit would have felt drained). Praying in the spirit, allows the beauty of Jesus to reflect through trials. The enemy always wants you to roll over and die, but no human being is worth you burying your life and destiny; (*2 Cor. 12:9-12*) God's strength is made perfect in our weakness. See (*Jer 29:11*)

The Reformation

We have a choice through trials, if we are going to agree with defeat or victory. We must never forget this scripture, (*Gen. 50:20*) as for you, you meant evil against me, but God meant it for my good. God will put the enemy to shame! (*1 Pet. 4:12-14*) The hardship we face in life is nothing compared to the Glory of God that will be rested on us (His Presence, His Grandeur, His Copiousness, His Splendor, and His Wealth). If those who tried to drag your life through the mud knew God's intent for your purpose and destiny, they wouldn't have. The devil should not have tried to embarrass you because it's predetermined that strong grace, favor and esteem is built in you. A win, win! Allow this scripture to resonate in your spirit **(Isaiah 35:4) - *"He will come and save you".*** This brings reassurance, embrace, and comfort from the sweetest comforter! God remembers you.

Prayer: Lord Jesus, help us to remain relevant and beautiful through trials and testing; knowing that you are touched by the feelings of our infirmity. Help us to behold the great and glorious outcome in your name, Amen.

19

Beautiful Appearance

I will praise you, because I am fearfully and wonderfully made' are the reassuring words of King David (*Psm. 139:14*). God's power is beyond human. He said I am God's omnipotent creation, knitted in my mother's womb, made wonderfully complex, while he was purposefully designing me with much loving care. He knew me! (1 *Pet. 2:9*) But ye are a chosen generation, a royal priesthood, a holy nation for his holy possession, that we may declare the praises of him who called us (while we were chosen to be royalty, nobility and powerful).

20

Beautiful Esther

Esther had beauty, she was lovely to look at, as she was fair and beautiful. We saw in the end how her qualities stood out (as she would have gone through the process of purification). I remembered when God told me "Esther has class and style". A woman of class is not just known for her wardrobe, but her behavior, mannerism, conduct, and her demeanor.

Speech Transformation

Esther's correlation with her Queenly principles stood out with such excellence, there were no signs of vulgarity or abrasiveness. Truth be told, it's sometimes hard to differentiate the saved from the unsaved. The speech patterns

and the brawl manifests through male and female. Suffice to say, we are all a work-in-progress, but In Christ we are new creatures. We have a responsibility to reflect Christ and the fruit of the Spirit. In the cases where Esther was threatened by Haman (in him seeking the destruction of the Jewish people), she diplomatically deployed her God given strategies that would allow him to fall in his own pit.

Work on the Attire

Esther had style. She was properly attired (especially when she was out). Style doesn't mean Gucci and Luis Vuitton. Though these are quality brands of garments, I absolutely think that Esther's appearance did not only have to do with clothing. I think there was a certain way she operated (how she played her role as a Queen).

Let's talk a little about modesty. It's the quality of not claiming attention to oneself (self-effacement). In society today, men and women are seeking so much attention with their kind of attire. I am not in a place to judge anyone, as I am a sinner saved by grace. But this scripture I know, (***1 Corinthians 10:31***) – ***"Whether therefore you eat, or drink, or whatsoever ye do, do all to the glory of God".*** Nowadays size doesn't matter anymore to some folks, but even our attire must be pleasing to God. Men and women with class and dignity know how to attire and be comforted in themselves. At the end of the day, we must live our lives to please God. It's a matter of constant self-attire introspection/self-analysis.

Warm and Welcoming

Stand out for God! That approach, that beautiful smile, hair nicely groomed, that sweet aroma, that modern etiquette, posture, mannerism and excellence. Note, I am not referring to a haughty and a proud look; but acquiring these wonderful attributes will help to enhance our presence at home and abroad. In my teenage years, I would constantly hear my mom quote these words, “If you don’t have looks, money or house, have manners and decency”. Manners I belief will take you places at times where money won’t. Teach the children! These qualities will help to polish their gifts and bring them before great men. Values have been depleted all over the world. But, a people that knows their God shall be strong and do exploits. Thank you, Jesus!

Prayer: Jesus, I thank you for creating us into your image. Help our appearance on all sides, to be pleasing to you. Cause your word to be the basis on how we represent you in Jesus’ Name, Amen.

21

Beautiful Deeds

Performing an action intentionally or consciously, in a positive way, has great rewards. Whatever you do in words or deeds, do all in the name of the Lord (*Col. 3:17*). It's mandatory for us to do good. **(Matthew 10:42) –** ***"And whosoever shall give … a cup of cold water only in the name of a disciple, verily I say unto you, he shall in no wise lose his reward."*** There are definitely great rewards when we do good.

It's incongruous if we avoid the principles of God's word to do good. Scripture tells us (*2 Cor. 9:8*) that his grace is abound towards us, that we may have all sufficiency in all things, an abundance unto every good work. Living the life of a Philanthropist absolutely brings satisfaction to me.

Helping along with my team to help students to head to University (who are not financially able to) and assisting the elderly and children of special needs, has ardently pushed me; that no matter what, always do the best you can. God will see about you with his copious abundance, to do more for those who are not able to. The five loaves and two fishes multiplied by the prayers of Jesus, was such a sign of compassion. He not only taught them, but also fed them.

Help!

The Good Samaritan! See (Luke 10:25-27)

Jesus gave the parable of the man who went down to Jericho. He was robbed and beaten and left for dead. The Priest and the Levites passed by and ignored him, but a Samaritan man felt compassion for him and helped him pour oil and bind up the wounds. How many times have we ignored the wounds and trouble of others in this life? Psalmist Helen Baylor sung this song – “See all the wounded, hear all their desperate cries for help. They’re pleading for shelter and for peace. Our comrades are suffering, come let us meet them at their needs, don’t let a wounded shoulder die.” Many have died because many have not taken the timeout to confront and deal with matters in love. God is depending on us to listen to their desperate cries. But instead, we turn a blind eye to their wounds, hurt and pain; we push matters aside or brush them under a carpet. Many times people need an outlet, to let it all out. Lives must be left with an indelible mark that will never be forgotten, of how they have received love and care from people with empathy and love.

Don’t mind if only a few return thanks! It was done to the glory of God.

Do it for others; It's done for you.

I remembered years ago I had planned a conference, and the venue cancelled us three days before the event. Truth be told, I panicked! Sat on my bed with teary eyes not knowing what to do, looking in space. Frustration had begun to creep in when suddenly, I felt the presence of God ushered over me. In the stillness of his voice, he said "How can I not come through for you? When I saw you had wound down your window while driving and aided to the street boys (whether or not your windshield was cleaned); You give to the street folks willingly."

Tears ran down my face as he called the name of a hotel to me. I'd never heard of that place before. I googled it, then went there and the place was available "Glory to God". We had a powerful time in God's presence. Such a move of God in that conference! (*Prov. 3:27-28*) Do not withhold good from those to whom it is due, when it's in your power to do, and to act. Don't say come back tomorrow! Be a beacon of hope and more hope.

22

Beautiful Feet

It is a great privilege when our steps are ordered by the Lord, even if we have to walk through storms and hardship. There is always a great sense of protection and assurance that God is in our midst. The scriptures says, **(Isaiah 52:7) "How beautiful and delightful are the feet of those who bring good news; Who announce peace, announce salvation, who say to Zion, "Your God Reigns";** Who God uses to settle matters, win souls, to tell of the one true mighty living God.

As it relates to your purpose and destiny, we have to make sure we are heading in the right direction that God has chosen while carrying beautiful feet; telling others that there is a perfect way out of their situation, and that way is through

Jesus Christ the Son of the living God. So many people are dying without knowing Christ. We need to keep on our foot geared to the gospel. The devil is busier than ever, seeking for blood. Therefore, movement is a must to counterattack the enemy and his schemes and plots. In these last days, we have to work assiduously to capture souls for Christ (prayerfully and purposefully).. God's love must be shown through us. It is that light that will captivate the heart, souls and mind of our loved ones (who are bound in chains and captivity) and lose them to accept the one who truly shed his blood for their sins, so they may live in him and serve him all their days.

Little Time

Time is of the essence. We are running out of time! The tribe of Issachar knew the times and seasons. With all the atrocities manifesting all over the globe, we are to be geared up! Suited up! Keep it moving with those gospel shoes! Satan has an all-out war, waging for the seeds. Allow the gospel to manifest among your unsaved families and friends. Every opportunity that we get to share Jesus Christ with others, we are definitely sowing seeds into their lives. Sometimes it may seem futile, but deep down the word is planted. Allow that passion in us to reach souls from becoming contaminated by condemnation, cynical behavior, pride, ignorance, talebearing and aggression. Allow the love of Jesus to be seen in us with all his wonders, compassion and purity. Let's become exemplary in spreading this beautiful gospel of peace. Whatever gifting Christ has laid on you, become a witness with a mission. John the Baptist used what he had to prepare the way for Christ. We are no lesser and should also prepare others for Christ great return.

Prayer: Jesus help us never to deny you but trust you to work with us to bring you to this lost and dying world. We thank you for grace in Jesus' name, Amen.

23

Beautiful thoughts

Of course the devil knows how to sow dirty seeds in the mind. Scripture tells us that **(2 Corinthians 10:4)** – ***"(the weapons of our warfare are not carnal, but mighty through God to the pulling down of strongholds;) Casting down imaginations, and every high thing that exalteth itself against the knowledge of God, and bringing into captivity every thought to the obedience of Christ;"*** We are to powerfully overturn strongly entrenched things; overturn reasoning and every lofty thing raised up against the knowledge of God. The devil appears every day with evil seeds to sow in the mind. A carnal mind is enmity/hostility with God. To be spiritually minded is Christlike; It's a battlefield and we must fight to win in our thoughts every day.

The mind is a combat zone. More and more we are encountering the dark side of ideology, in such deceptive form. Men's appetite are for human blood and sacrifice; The thoughts are so warped that lives matter no more (the dogmatic belief system has blinded the concept of life's values and as a result amity is seldomly found through society).

We eat, drink and laugh with one another, but knives are always present to cut throat, along with a stab in the back (metaphorically speaking). The Legend Bob Marley sang "Emancipate yourself from mental slavery, none but ourselves can free our minds!" (Jesus took that mental curse upon himself). (*Gal. 3:13-14*) Christ has redeemed us from the curse of the law, being made a curse for us: for it is written, Cursed is everyone that hangs on a tree, that the blessing of Abraham might come to the Gentiles through

Jesus Christ. He gave us the resurrection power exchange (The mind of Christ).

Wake up!

(*Phil. 4:8*) Whatsoever things are pure, true, honest, or of good report; if there be any virtue or praise, think on these things. The truth we know will set us free. (*Isa. 26:3*) He whose thoughts are stayed on Christ, he will keep your heart in perfect peace. Gird of the loins of your mind (just as how you use a belt to gird/tighten the waist). In the same breath, tighten the mind with the word of God. Think positive, think good, think just! (*Prov. 23:7*) For as a man thinketh so is he. Think great! Think success! Think purposeful! Think goodness! Think forward! Think peace! Think overcoming! Think better! Think sound!

Prayer: Lord help those who don't know you to give you a chance in their lives, so that their way of thinking can be altered through Jesus Christ. For those of us who know you, you give the will power to maintain a good thought life through the help of your Holy Spirit, Amen!

24

Beautiful Times

Amidst the act of savagery and difficult times, during the pandemic; It was a poignant regrettable and very sad moment. The reality stood out, that many since then have bounced back somewhat to normal living and, of course, trying to make do with what is present. Many lives were loss, and the grief still lingers; But (*Ecc. 3:11*) in his time, he makes all things beautiful. God holds the world in his hands and have brought beautiful comfort from his word to many; and with that we praise his holy name.

No Future Fear

This woman that was described in the book of Proverbs as virtuous, is a woman that never existed. But the writer gave an immaculate description of what a virtuous woman's character should entail. In Prov. 31:25, she is clothed with strength and dignity, and she laughs without fear of the future. These times we are living in, somewhat can be scary. **(2 Timothy 1:7) – *"For God hath not given us the spirit of fear; but of power, and of love, and of a sound mind".*** (*Col. 1:27*) Christ in us the hope of Glory; We therefore have to trust God and live everyday like it is the last day. God has our bright future in his hand.

One day there will be no more sorrow, no more heartaches, pain or evil. All tears will be wiped away and all things will be beautiful again. He has orchestrated beautiful times for us here on earth, and not even the devil can stop it! Jesus was a man of sorrow (acquainted with grief), but the veil was rend when he bled and died, that while we are here we have access to joy, peace, happiness, hope and love. His love is commended to us that while we were yet sinners, he died for us. Thank you, Jesus! Help us to acknowledge your orchestrated beautiful times. Remind us that you have this whole world in your hand, as well as our laughter, our joy, our peace of mind, our comfort, and your goodness, Amen.

The Attraction

What you expect in life, is automatically (sometimes) what you will receive. You have to have sight beyond your open eyes. It is important to not just look at what we see and make hasty decisions, but first see through the eyes of the Spirit and believe in God's word that there is more to life than what we see with our eyes. "But as it is written, Eye hath not seen, nor ear heard, neither have entered into the heart of man, the things which God hath prepared for them that love him." 1

Corinthians 2:9. Just remember that God is the Architect; he clearly knows how to remodel a disfigured situation. Sometimes it's the odyssey of the process which seems unbearable, but "Timing is everything"! God is undressing you from the cliche apparatus and allowing you to become incited with originality. In God's beautiful timing, you will be phenomenal, extraordinary and filled with memorable moments of bliss.

I prophesy - That grace, power, favor, and breakthrough will be your allotment. That family relationships will be healed, your children will serve God, you will be debt free, that business will bud, that abundance will be visible, and you will lay foundations for building. That gift is about to make room for you, that big door will open for you, your anointing will increase, wisdom will go before you, your mind will be strengthened, your red carpet will roll out, you will rise over the attacks and attackers, and God will bruise the enemy under your feet – SHORTLY! You are about to travail and give birth to "Beautiful Times"

25

Beautiful Discernment

Being able to discern by the Spirit of God, is a beautiful experience. One of the reasons are because (*1 Cor. 1:29*) no flesh shall glory in his presence. The root meaning for discernment (Greek: diakrisis and diakrino) is to divide ("dia") and to judge ("krino"). It's the ability to obtain sharp perception, or to judge well (knowing the difference between right or wrong, good or evil). **(Proverbs 3:5-6) – *"Trust in the Lord with all thine heart; and lean not unto thine own understanding. In all thy ways acknowledge him, and he shall direct thy paths."*** (not being reliant on our own abilities). In Philippians 1: 9-10 the Apostle Paul encourages believers to develop a discerning Spirit ***"And this I pray, that your love may abound yet more and more in knowledge and in all judgement;"*** (dept of

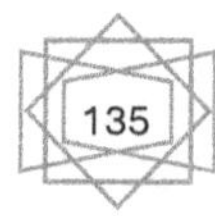

insight), so that you may be able to discern and manifest perspicacity (a ready insight into things).

Discernment is linked to love, knowledge and pursuing what is mindfully excellent.

Fooled Once

Years ago, my husband and I pastored our first church in rural Hanover, Jamaica. And of course, I was always that city girl who would find this transition quite arduous. We had started to build relationships with a few Pastors, while we were still trying to adjust. There were two sweet-spirited Pastors who were having a revival at their church with an Evangelist who was in her sixties along with her granddaughter. They introduced her to us, as an anointed vessel who was filled with the word of God while we visited the meetings. We were quite excited to invite her to our church, after she would have finished the Revival.

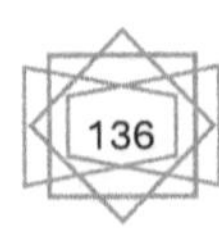

We lived in an area where no hotels or guest houses were nearby. So, we eventually had to do the hosting at our home. Our hearts were moved with compassion, as she seemed to be quite passionate about God and the things of God. She graced the platform with beautiful singing and teaching the word of God. The first five days everything seemed to be going good until the service took a turn. My husband had started to see her ministration manifesting without love. She had begun to get real harsh with the congregation, and pronounced some real judgment there.

Before she came to us, I was praying to God for a spiritual mom, so when she came, I held on to the fact that God had answered my prayers. It had become a nightmare in our home, because I had already developed an evil soul tie with this woman. Her manipulation and control took ahold of me (as I was no longer myself). Two weeks turned into months. I would sit by this woman's door every night as she opened her Bible to share or just share other things. One thing she kept saying was that "God brought me here for you and wants me to mentor you". At nights when I should be in bed beside my husband, I was at her door. I became her slave, yet still my husband would not say one word. This woman's ministry was so flawed, and I just could not see it.

I had begun to realize the more, that I was not feeling or looking like me. I could not perform my marital duties or house duties. As the mornings came, I would do breakfast and was back at her doorstep engaged in her conversations. The look of a Zombie was all over me saints, and my prayer life was in trouble. A few of our members saw her flawed character but kept quiet as she was getting worse. My husband then decided to step in by way of confronting her. Her pride got in the way, in so much that she could not accept the correction. She was exacerbated in her response, and she told me that God would deal with anyone who challenges her, and that he was going to kill my husband. And of course I believed, because my mind became very passive, and I could not control my thoughts (the level of how I was oppressed also bothered me). My spouse asked her kindly to leave. She left, but here came the consequences for my naivety.

A new chapter had begun called cleansing! But first I asked my husband, why did he not say anything during the time. He remarked "I was just watching to see if you would wake up!" I felt violated by this woman and tricked. Folks I had to go through deliverance for two months in a row (every morning at a certain time). It was mandated by God, whether I liked it or not. It was very hard, but I had to learn my lesson. I was finally freed and asked the Lord why he had allowed it. He replied, "Maxine you did not ask me if she was the Spiritual Mom I sent you". That got me way down in my soul and I cried profusely, repented, and felt like I was walking on a cloud. GLORY HALLELUJAH!

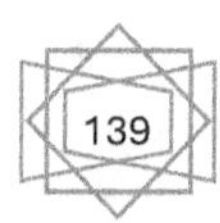

Since then, God has graced me with the gift of Discerning of spirits (seeing both Angels and demons), mentoring many folks and watching them grow in God's Grace and Love. Beloved, try every spirit; See whether they be of God. *See 1 John 4:1-5.*

Wrong Perception

There is this old-time proverb that says, "once bitten, twice shy". With unpleasant situations in the past, you would not want history to repeat itself. There once was this situation, where Jim had a dream concerning two youngsters joining hands in marriage. I thought it would be good since they went to the same Church, sitting under mentorship. The young lady had spoken to me on numerous occasions, that she felt like God was pulling Steve to her. For me, it was always a pleasure to see young people tie the knot as God leads. I supposed she had mentioned the same thing to Jim. I just felt excited! There were a few marriages that God had me confirm, and until this day, the couples are still together "Praise the LORD"

So, during this time I was the Senior Pastor at my church, and one Sunday morning I was ministering in worship, and I felt the presence of God very rich (so much that no preaching could go on). While I was in worship, I had this open vision. It was very quick, and I saw as it were Sarah and Steve coming together to join hands in holy matrimony. I suddenly snaped out of it and opened my mouth in their presence. I remembered saying something like this "make contact after church". They eventually made contact and started dating for a while, then they broke off the relationship. I ask God what happened, and no answer came, but then I pondered to myself; It seemed that I had Jim's dream in my head (maybe my subconscious). Thoughts began to bombard my mind and I could only come to the conclusion that I had blundered. I

felt bad because I always pray for my flesh to subside and submit to the prophetic. With all of this being said, it teaches us to try the spirit to see if it is of God (*1 John 4*).

Today Steve has found his wife. I spoke a word into Steve's life about a connection and the word came to pass, and through that door he met his wife. It's imperative to become quite sentient, being able to discern and perceive things. Each journey is a learning curve in life to be better and to be able to please God and to enhance the lives of others through right judgment. Beautiful Discernment manifests by the Holy Spirit. It's birthed out of a life of prayer, consecration, love and wisdom. Ask God today to allow you to discern beautifully. (*Luke 11:11*) If you ask him for bread, you will not be given a stone, if you ask him for a fish, you will not get a serpent. He is God almighty! He lives, he reigns, majestic and magnificent for evermore.

Biography

Apostle Maxine Gordon

Apostle Maxine Gordon, Peace Ambassador, UN, is the founder and CEO of "Heaven Blazing Earth Charity", which governs HBEMI's charity scholarship fund and the "Feed The 5,000" feeding programme. She is an idealistic person who cherishes goals, values, and dreams and also is a philanthropist at heart. With her giving, caring, donating, and seeking to look out for the welfare of persons, she has a strong passion for the poor and the needy and as such, birthed this HBEMI outreach ministry and charity.

Apostle Gordon is also the founder of "Woman Into Diamond", a platform enabling and impacting women to fulfill their God-given Purpose all over the Globe. She has also co-founded New Covenant Ministries International with her husband, Apostle Dr. Richardo Gordon, and is a supporting wife and a loving mother of four children: Shereca, Kurtlando, John, and Destinique, residing with her family in Highgate, St. Mary, Jamaica, W.I.

Being an accomplished Psalmist, Author, Song Writer, Recording Artiste, and Poet, Apostle Maxine

Gordon has written over 600 songs and some of her notable and acclaimed works include the soul touching, "I Am A Winner" album and her literary breakthrough soul-searching study books, "Treasury Of A Lifetime" and "Pure Gems Of Glory". She is an International Business Woman and can be likened to the "Virtuous Woman" described in Proverbs 31.

Apostle Gordon has also been the recipient of Heavenly Downloads for course modules such as "The Glory of God", "The Fire of God", "The Call of God", "Understanding Prophetic Worship", "Angels, Healing & Miracles, Signs & Wonders", and "Advancing the Kingdom in Intercession". These courses take every participant on a life-changing journey in their relationship with God.

Though she is in full-time ministry, Apostle Gordon has traveled both nationally and internationally, ministering the Undiluted Word of God from the platform of Maxine Gordon Ministries. She has offered spiritual and emotional healing, as she guides persons in transforming their inner selves, and has also led many women into deeper, more fulfilling prayer and worshipful lives through her own epiphanies in the area.

Ministering with a strong prophetic mantle accompanied by deliverance, uncommon signs and wonders follow her ministry. She is known as a no-

nonsense Preacher and a Holiness Prophet. Powerful, anointed trumpets resound from her belly, which creates spiritual atmospheres and mighty explosions, which often cause people to weep and shake heavily as she ministers.

BOOKS BY THE AUTHOR

PROPHETIC WORSHIP

Module Book

Course Objectives

(1) This Course will give a practical understanding of prophetic worship.

(2) students will receive biblical revelation coupled with personal experience to show a pathway to prophetic worship.

(3) Students will be equipped with the knowledge of how to enter God's presence and lead others into it.

(4) Students will be given the practical tools of how to push in the glory and pull out divine provision both privately and publically.

(5) This study will provoke a craving for the manifest presence of God and for more of the spirit .

(6) Students at the end of the course will be able to quantify what they learned through questions and answers.

THE GLORY OF GOD

Module Book

Course Objectives

(1) This Course was designed to take you into Dimension of God's Glory.

(2) You will develop a hunger and passion to see God's Glory.

(3) You will be equipped on how to pull on God's Glory.

(4) You will receive revelation through God's Word.

(5) You will become a Glory Carrier.

(6) Glorious manifestation will become the order of your day.

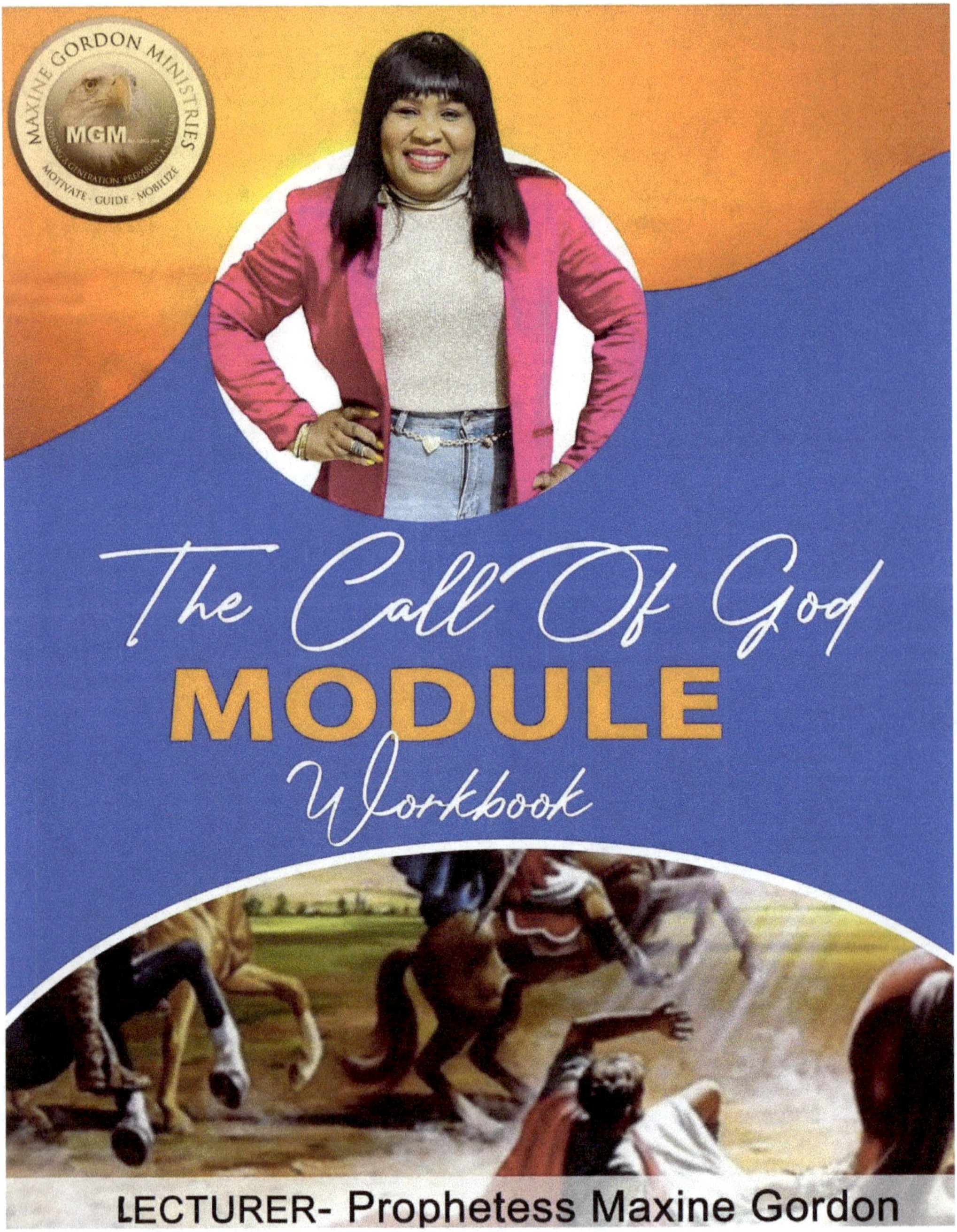

MAXINE GORDON MINISTRIES

MGM

INSPIRING A GENERATION. PREPARING A NATION

MOTIVATE · GUIDE · MOBILIZE

The Call Of God

MODULE

Workbook

LECTURER- Prophetess Maxine Gordon

The Fire of God
Module Course

Lecturer *Rev. Prophetess Maxine Gordon*

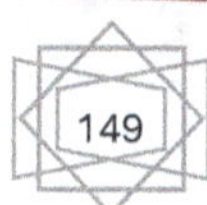

PROPHETIC WORSHIP
MODULE COURSE
WORK BOOK

LECTURER: REV. MAXINE GORDON

MAXINE GORDON MINISTRIES

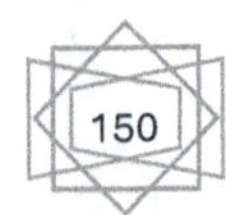

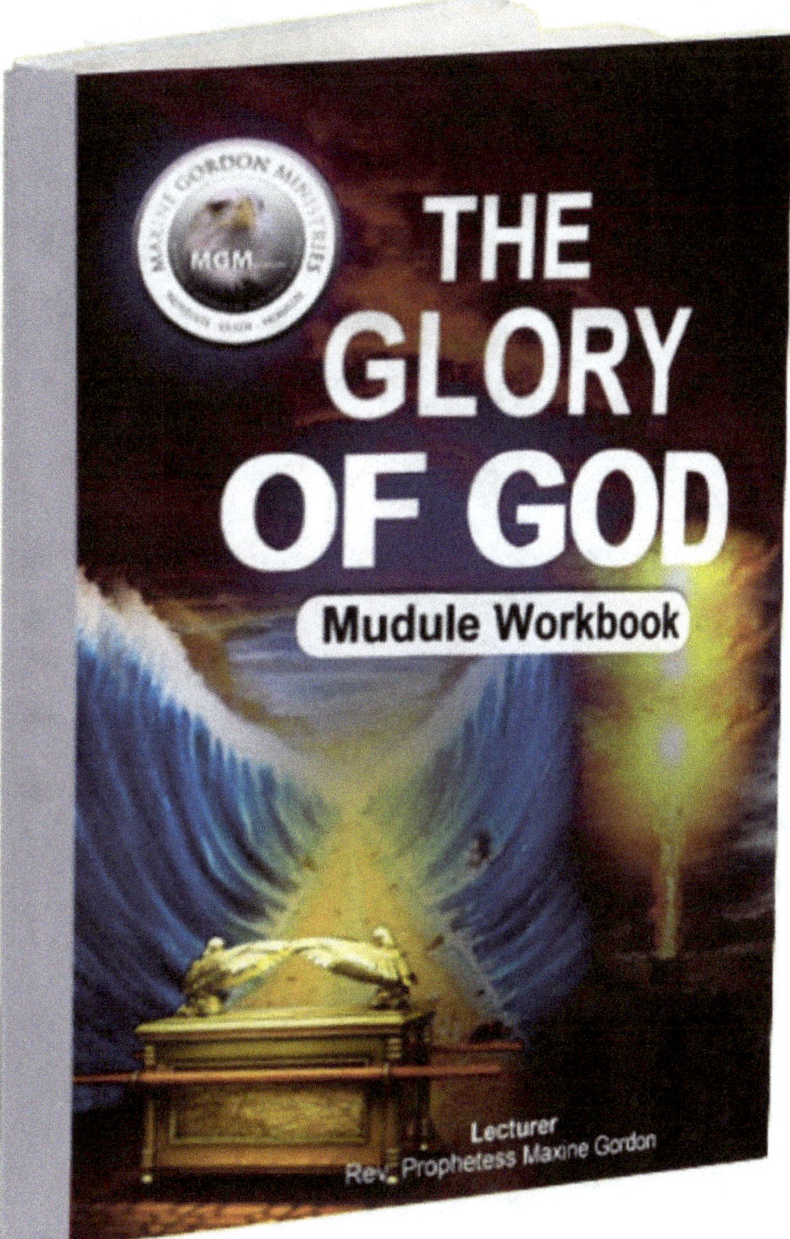
MGM
THE
GLORY
OF GOD
Mudule Workbook
Lecturer
Rev. Prophetess Maxine Gordon

PROPHETESS MAXINE GORDON

Pure Gems of Glory

POEMS, QUESTIONNAIRES & PROPHETIC DECLARATIONS

Pure Gems of Glory

First and foremost this book is a must read that will bring about great changes in your life. As the reader you will experience the hand of Jehovah God heavy upon you. It will promote divine transformation and turn around for you and angels of God that are assigned to you will begin to work on your behalf speedily and bring release as you receive tools that put angels to work. The principles found in this book are Biblical and will bring about sanctification, deliverance and healing even a new beginning in your life. As you read anticipate the blessing of the Lord from the crown of your head to the soles of your feet cause after you have suffered awhile you can only reflect His glory.

NOTES

NOTES

NOTES

NOTES

www.ingramcontent.com/pod-product-compliance
Lightning Source LLC
LaVergne TN
LVHW010903110826
845149LV00005B/1457

* 9 7 9 8 9 9 8 8 5 1 6 3 6 *